WATER GARDENING

WATER GARDENING

Ethne Clarke

WITH A FOREWORD BY
MAX DAVIDSON

SUNBURST BOOKS

This edition first published in 1995 by
Sunburst Books,
Deacon House,
65 Old Church Street,
London SW3 5BS.

ISBN 1 85778 170 8

Publishing Manager *Casey Horton*
Editor *Paul Brewer*
Designer *Ming Cheung*

Publisher's Note
Readers should note that plant breeders introduce new cultivars all the time.
Please check your seed catalogues for the latest ones.

```
WARNING
If using chemical
herbicides, fungicides or insecticides,
be sure to follow exactly
the manufacturer's instructions.
```

Printed and bound in Hong Kong

CONTENTS

FOREWORD 6

INTRODUCTION 7

TYPES OF WATER GARDEN 8
    Choosing the Site 10
    Water Garden Extras 14

MAKING A WATER GARDEN 20
    Bog Gardens Made with Flexible Liners 24
    Ponds Made with Rigid Liners 26

WATERFALLS 28

HALF-BARREL CONTAINER WATER GARDEN 30

CONCRETE POOLS 32

PLANTING 34
    Practicalities of Planting 38

CARE AND MAINTENANCE 42
    Safety 47

WATER GARDEN PLANTS 48

INDEX 63

FOREWORD

There is something in human nature that finds the sights and sounds of water in the garden a soothing feature. Water in the form of a pool or a fountain can transform the view through your window from a pedestrian prospect like that of the Jones's next door into a splendid spectacle that will be the envy of your street. Aquatic plants are among the loveliest of all flowers, with delicate, intriguing stems and roots. And they may not be as troublesome to grow as you might imagine. Water lilies may look exotic, but the latest hardy varieties will thrive virtually anywhere. Their colours will certainly impress: pure white, yellow, pink, apricot, orange or red.

There is an enormous number of possibilities for improving the appearance and enjoyment of your gardening by adding water features. The work of building a pool has never been easier. By making use of the latest construction techniques, you could install one in your garden in just two weekends. You simply dig a hole and line it to make it watertight with, typically, a sheet of black butyl rubber. Today's pond liners are of such a high quality that they usually carry a 20-year guarantee and are expected to last for 50 years.

A pool can be surrounded by paving, or constructed so that part of the soil around it remains permanently damp, to let you grow bog plants such as astilbes, irises and primulas, as well as plants with magnificent leaves such as ligularias, rheums and rodgersias – if you have room for these gigantic plants. In the pool itself, in addition to water lilies, you can have deep water and marginal flowering plants, with just their 'feet' in the water, and all sorts of reeds. The soil from your excavation can be used to make a rockery with a small waterfall.

Once the pool is installed, you open your water garden of colourful plants to all sorts of exciting possibilities, such as having a fountain and a waterfall, as well as fish. The pumps that power fountains and waterfalls have also been engineered for safety and low-cost running. Most can even be immersed in the pool.

Fish are indeed one of the great attractions of water gardening. The choice ranges from the common goldfish to the more exotic shubunkins, comets and golden orfe, and the expensive Japanese Koi carp. Some garden centres also sell fish. The alternative is to order them from a specialist firm which will normally get them to you by next-day delivery.

Water gardening doesn't require a great deal of space. Aquatic tub kits enable you to grow some lovely water lilies and other plants in conservatories, patios and tiny gardens.

Most garden centres have water sections where you can buy all you need, or you can order an entire kit from one of the specialist water gardening firms. You can buy precast glass fibre waterfall and rivulet units. There is a large choice of waterfall kits and fountain spray patterns so that your pool can match our own ideas. You could even add a set of colour-changing lights to illuminate the fountain by night.

Water really does make a garden sparkle. It could be just that special touch of magic your garden needs.

MAX DAVIDSON

INTRODUCTION

Water has been an ornamental feature in gardens since earliest times. Tomb paintings from the Egyptian pyramids show that the Pharaohs enjoyed lotus pools, canals and rills, fountains and cascades. Similar evidence exists in delightful Persian miniatures showing paradise gardens, representing the perfect world at the dawn of creation, where water was as important as flowers and fruit trees. Among the eerily preserved remains of the ancient Roman city of Pompeii are the gardens of important citizens where water played through formal groves of box, bay and rose trees in marble-lined channels.

Water gardens really came into their own during the Italian Renaissance, and particularly in the magnificent palace and villa gardens in the hills of Frascati outside Rome. But the most superb example of the Italian mastery of water hydraulics is the garden of the Villa d'Este. From the palatial villa at the summit of the hill, water cascades down through the terraced garden in a series of formal pools, fountains and waterfalls. The force of the descending water creates enough pressure to play fantastic organs, the air being forced through the pipes by the rush of water. Similar to this is the water theatre at the Villa Aldobrandini, where the air currents created by the cascading water were harnessed and channelled through a small hole in the floor of a garden room. A brass ball was suspended in this stream, held aloft by thin air! It was one of the marvels of Renaissance garden ornament.

Then there were the fabulous gardens of Louis XIV of France, the Sun King, at his palace Versailles. Created in the late 17th century its grounds are threaded through with formal canals and pools on which Louis staged some of his most extravagant entertainments; full battle scenes were enacted between rival 'fleets'. There were fountains galore, and countless other smaller water features animating the garden's strict formality.

Not to be outdone, some of the great noble families of England installed water features, less extravagant than their Continental counterparts, perhaps, but none the less enchanting. The great Cascade at Chatsworth is probably the most noteworthy. The formality of the 17th century was followed in the 18th century by what was meant to be a return to nature, with landscape artists such as Capability Brown altering the course of rivers and excavating ornamental lakes in order to improve on nature – as though nature needed help!

Water has never been far from the centre of garden-makers' attention; Gertrude Jekyll and Sir Edwin Lutyens collaborated on some delightful rills and pools as central features in their garden schemes. In our own time, Sir Geoffrey Jellicoe has continued the tradition: the musical cascade in the garden at Shute House, Dorset, is a charming and lyrical addition to a thought-provoking design.

Water soothes by its coolness, enchants with the reflection of light on its rippled surface and playfully animates with the music of its splash and gurgle. If you are making a garden, try to include water in the plan. It can be as simple a thing as a half-barrel filled with water and planted with a single water lily. You won't regret it, and you'll be making your own contribution to the continuation of an historic gardening skill.

Types of Water Garden

THERE ARE MANY DIFFERENT TYPES of material and methods of construction for water features in a garden. Pools are the most common choice and traditionally were made of concrete. These are nearly always formal in design, assuming a geometric shape – circle, square, oblong and so on. Often a fountain, perhaps functioning as a dramatic centrepiece, would be included in the design.

Informal ponds are most often irregular in shape and are designed to blend naturally with surrounding gardens and landscape. The earliest of these sorts of pond were made using preformed rigid, yet irregularly shaped, liners made of plastic or fibreglass. Often they were coloured a lurid swimming-pool turquoise, highly inappropriate for anyone trying to create a pond with a natural appearance. Using a rigid liner is quite a quick and easy way to create a water feature. They are still widely used today, but thankfully manufacturers have improved the colouring, and most are tinted a dark, muddy neutral shade.

Flexible liners are probably the most popular method for making informal, irregularly shaped pools. It is possible to make a pool of any shape or size using a flexible liner – although good-quality ones are not cheap. By using a rigid liner to create a cascade, or by covering stepped excavations with the flexible liner, you will be able to combine a water garden with a rock garden, or to create a mini-waterfall.

Natural water gardens, if you are fortunate enough to have a pond or stream within your garden, require no special liners or construction methods, and involve only the simple, unobtrusive cultivation of the plants along the water's edge.

ABOVE: Well begun — a natural stream makes creating a water garden a task half done.

RIGHT: The fanciful combination of natural and artificial objects reveals a lot about a gardener's design skills.

LEFT: **Raising a pond heightens the artificiality of the design, so a formal geometric shape bordered in with bricks would be appropriate.**

BELOW: **Paving stones used on the patio also edge the pool and form a path to the rest of the garden.**

Choosing the Site

Before embarking on pool-making, there are a few considerations that must be evaluated if you hope for any measure of success.

It is a fact of nature that water flows downhill, and that it settles in the lowest level of the landscape. The lesson here is, don't put the pond at the top of a hill or even a slight incline. It will never look right. You may be able to get away with placing the pool wherever you like if the slope is almost imperceptible, as it is in my seemingly flat Norfolk garden. Nevertheless, there is a slope, and I don't think I would feel entirely comfortable with a pool that was anywhere else except at the lowest point of this gentle incline.

If the water feature is going to be located quite near the house it should be designed to fit in with the 'architectural' surroundings, perhaps by setting it in the paving of the patio, or by creating it as a raised water garden using the same brick or stonework as in the

ABOVE: A waterfall effect is achieved in this container water garden by combining a fountain and clematis climbers.

structure of the house. The planting within it can be as lush and natural-looking as you like, but do try to make the pool seem part of its setting.

Similarly, if you aim to make a wildlife pond, emulating a natural water feature, avoid straight, hard edges. William Robinson, the maestro of the wild garden, was spot-on when he wrote, 'Nature abhors a straight line.' The best source of inspiration is a genuine pond; study how it fits into the landscape – see how the plants grow in and around it.

The final appearance of the pool will be directly related to the trouble you take constructing it. Perhaps the biggest mistake DIY water gardeners make is excavating the hole, and then banking up the soil and rocks and rubble they take from it all around its perimeter. The end result looks

like a bomb crater. So be sure you have somewhere to dispose of the spoil – and there will be quite a bit of it, even from the smallest hole.

ABOVE: **A Japanese-style garden.**
BELOW: **Acclimatising goldfish.**

You must consider the needs of the plants that will grow in your pool. Plants for a water garden are of three sorts: *submerged*, with their roots in the pool bottom and their leafy growth submerged below the water line; *floating*, with roots in the water and greenery floating freely around the pool; and *aquatic*, with roots in the pool bottom and leaves and flowers floating on the water surface. For example, water lilies are aquatic, duckweed is floating and elodea is submerged. Besides their obvious need for a constant supply of water, during the growing season the plants in your pool need direct sunlight for most of the day. So avoid locating the pool in places shaded by neighbouring buildings, trees, hedges and so on.

Plants also need space, so you should make the pool as big as possible (without submerging the whole garden!) and 45-60 cm/18-24 in deep, at the least. Water absorbs the sun's energy efficiently and a shallow pool will warm up quickly, creating an ideal environment for algae but a poor one for plants and fish. For this reason, water gardens in warmer areas, such as the southwest of Britain, should be dug deeper; in other regions you can provide a 'deep-end', a small section at least 30 cm/12 in deeper than the rest of the pool, to keep the pool's overall temperature just right.

Another very good reason *not* to place a pool or pond near trees is that autumn leaves are as bad for water as they are for gardens and lawns, releasing noxious gases into the water as they rot, poisoning the fish and setting up trouble for the following season. Beware, too, of plants with toxic berries such as yew and laburnum.

BELOW: **A well-managed wild pond will support an amazing variety of flora and fauna.**

Water Garden Extras

Fountains, waterfalls, artificial rills and streams must be powered by pumps. They fall into two categories, submerged and surface, determined by where they are installed. Submerged pumps are located below the water line, they run silently and all their leads and connectors are disguised by the hard landscaping around the pool. There is a wide range available so you should be able to select the one that best suits the task, moving the water through fountain jets, circulating it from cascade to pool and back again, or even generating the flow or a gentle stream. Submerged pumps are suitable for most small- to medium-sized water garden features.

Surface pumps are used for large-scale features and are located apart from the water garden. One surface pump can be used to power the water flow through a number of fountains, cascades and so on.

Even if you don't have room for a pond, you should be able to find space

ABOVE: The shape of the flag irises echo the fountain's spray.
RIGHT: Circular-spray fountain.
BELOW: A simple jet.

ABOVE: Sculpted fountains can add an extra dimension to the garden water feature.

LEFT: You can achieve an air of mystery by obscuring a fountain, such as this colourful mosaic one, with reeds.

for a fountain. There are fountains that send a trickle of water from a wall-fixed ornament into a basin, and simple jets that spout from shallow containers such as a terracotta urn or trough. You can even fix a spray fountain into a half-barrel. City-dwellers would find any of these suitable for a patio or terrace garden.

However, there are a few things to bear in mind; if the garden is open to the prevailing winds, on a breezy day a fine spray will blow away, so

use a bubbler fountain or one that produces large water drops. Keep the size of the jet in proportion to the pool from which it sprays; its height should be about half the width of the pool. Locate the fountain away from water plants, which will not enjoy a constant pummelling from falling water; for neighbouring beds and borders, select plants that will appreciate the humid microclimate created by the evaporating water of nearby fountains and pools.

Lighting can be used to good effect with pools and fountains, their beams aimed to reflect from the water's surface or to catch the sparkle of a trickling water jet. Lights can also be submerged to illuminate the water and plants from below – although the effect can appear rather extraterrestrial unless carefully planned.

WARNING Unless you are a professional electrician or superconfident about your DIY skills in this area, call in a professional to advise about and install any electrical feature. Water and electricty are lethal in combination.

ABOVE: A mask-and-basin is a traditional style well-suited to old-fashioned gardens.

RIGHT: This fountain is placed to act as a focal point at the end of a garden vista.

BELOW: A humorous touch won't go amiss.

MAKING A WATER GARDEN

BY USING A FLEXIBLE LINER you can create a delightful curvaceous pool with stepped edges and boggy margins to take herbaceous plants that like to have their toes in water, as well as a wide range of water plants. Liners are made of either polythene, PVC or butyl sheeting. Butyl is the more expensive of the three materials; it has the longest life span, being impervious to the effects of ultraviolet rays. When you make your purchase, ask the dealer about its quality, guarantees and so on. PVC is mid-range in price and durability, while polythene is inexpensive in the short-term, but is soon degraded by ultraviolet rays.

ABOVE: The natural look is the aim of an informal pool.

RIGHT: Camouflaged stepping stones mimic the broad, flat leaves of the Nymphaea.

Choose your site carefully, as described earlier. Use a suitable length of garden hose to lay out the design. Shape it into graceful curves and do not make them too tight. Avoid any sharp angles: it is very tricky to smooth the liner into such formations. Also, slowly developing curves look more natural. Use the edge of your spade to slice the outline into the turf.

To determine the size of liner you will need, measure the length of the pool, then add twice the eventual depth, plus 30 cm/12 in; measure the width, add twice the eventual depth plus 30 cm/12 in. To be extra confident of having enough liner to cover, you can add 60 cm/24 in instead of 30 cm/12 in.

Skim the turf off the pool area (stack it upside down out of the way to rot down for compost). Methodically excavate the hole, taking care to make shallow, sloping stepped sides on which to stand pots of aquatic

plants. Endeavour to keep the sides level with each other by checking with a carpenter's level across the width and length of the pool; you do not want one edge to have several inches of liner showing above the water line, while the opposite bank sits level.

Line the completed hole with a minimum of 2.5 cm/1 in of sand over which you can lay old mattresses, carpets, layers of old newspapers – anything that will provide a cushion between the bare earth and the liner. Rocks and rubble would eventually break through the liner from below, while sharp objects dropped into the pool, or uninvited guests such as pets, could puncture it from above.

Beginning at one end, unfold the liner across the pool, letting it drape into the excavation. Smooth the liner into the curves, neatly pleating and tucking as necessary. As the liner takes the shape of the pool, hold the upper edges in place with heavy weights (bricks, rocks, etc.). Stand back from time to time to check the evenness of your progress; it's easier to make adjustments as you work rather than when the liner is completely unfolded and spread out.

When you are satisfied with the cover, fill the pool with water. Do this slowly; shift the weights securing the sides as the weight of water settles and stretches the liner into the shape of the hole.

The last step is to trim the edges of the liner to about 40 cm/8 in all round. Don't trim it too closely or the liner edge may sink into the pond. Dig in the edge and then lay paving stones all round the edge of the pool,

LEFT: Koi carp come in a wide variety of colours, and are best suited to large pools.

and allowing them to overhang the water's edge by a few centimetres. Bed the pavers into a two-to-one sand/cement mix, and then seal the joins between them with cement.

Even if you are extremely cautious when preparing the bed for the liner, tears and holes can appear. Tree roots, for example, have a great proficiency for poking through liners (another reason not to locate a water garden near trees). Also natural deterioration will weaken the liners. There are repair kits available for pool liners; be sure to follow the instructions exactly and make the patch at least once again as large as the damaged area. Don't stint on the repair; you may only have to do it again.

BELOW: On the margin of this large pond are elephant weed, astilbes and pickerel weed.

Bog Gardens Made with Flexible Liners

Bog gardens accommodate plants that enjoy permanently moist, but not sodden soil. They look especially well if located adjacent to a pool and can be incorporated into the surrounding landscape using pebbles, pavers or other hard-landscaping details.

Bog gardens are treated in a slightly different way to other pools made with a flexible liner. First, it isn't necessary to cushion the liner. You must also pierce through the liner across its entire surface to allow a modicum of drainage. Use the garden fork to do this, spacing the punctures about 1m/3 ft apart. To prepare the bog garden, dig a shallow hole with the sides slightly sloping, so that the level of the bog garden where it meets the edge of the pool is lower than the water of the pool. Spread a 5 cm/2 in layer of washed gravel in the bottom of the hole and then fill with soil containing a high level of water-retaining humus. You can increase the water-holding capacity of your garden soil by incorporating plenty of peat and well-rotted compost.

Smooth pebbles and gravel should be arranged around the edge of the bog garden in as natural a manner as possible, mixing grades and textures for a random effect.

Throughout the year, keep a check on the moisture level of the soil, topping up the water in the pool if too much is leaching out into the bog garden. If the soil is soupy or like porridge, it is too wet. This can be remedied by piercing more holes in the liner. If you have graded the sides of the bog garden pit so that the soil level is shallower than in the centre, or else created a stepped area along one edge of the bog, you will find that the shallower area dries more quickly than the deeper areas. Some plants do like it wetter than others so be sure to take this into consideration. Many ornamental grasses, such as *Miscanthus* species, like wet conditions, as do some ferns including *Osmunda cinnamomea*, the cinnamon fern. Many of the primroses, *Primula japonica*, for example, relish having damp toes, as do the yellow flag irises, *Iris pseudoacorus*. Hostas, ligularia, ornamental rhubarbs and the magnificent *Gunnera manicata* are foliage plants that can be combined to create some dramatic planting schemes.

ABOVE: A pool forms the centrepiece of this bog garden.
RIGHT: A bog garden can act as a transitional zone between a pond and the lawn.
BELOW: Make sure that the level of your pool is higher than that of your bog garden.

Look too at the form of the plants. Anything with a weeping habit will appear especially graceful trailing above the water's edge.

In the pond itself you can plant a huge variety of

aquatics, and in an informal pool you mustn't stint. There is quite a long list to choose from: rushes, grasses, water lilies, duckweed – but only the common or lesser sorts – and water chestnut.

Additionally, the combination of informal pool and bog garden provides the perfect habitat for a range of water-loving wildlife.

Ponds Made with Rigid Liners

Rigid liners are formed from plastic, either as a plain or reinforced plastic shell, and from glass fibre. The former

ABOVE: Water lilies, marigolds and sweet flag iris feature in this kidney bean-shaped pool.

are the least expensive as they are less durable and deteriorate rapidly when exposed to sun. Therefore it is vital that all the exposed edges of the pool be covered with pavers and the water level maintained so that the plastic surfaces are kept protected from the sun. Glass fibre is impervious to ultraviolet, so a good choice for the construction of waterfalls, which is what moulded rigid liners are most often used for, but this can only be successfully done where there is a natural slope in the garden, or where excavation has altered the contours to create natural-looking slopes.

It can be rather a fiddle getting the liner to sit properly in the hole which you have excavated, but it is worth getting it right, since any unevenness would cause stresses on the liner leading eventually to cracks and splits. The easiest way to ensure a good fit is to make a paper template. Tape together sheets of newspaper to make a single sheet large enough to cover the liner. Turn the liner over on to the paper and trace its outline. Measure the width of any shelves and draw a line indicating their position within the pool. Measure the depth laying a cane across the pool and holding a ruler against it to take the measurements from the bottom and at the shelves. Make a note of these as you go.

Cut out the template and make slits along the markings for the shelf positions and the bottom of the pool. Because the pool was upside down to make the tracing, the template must be turned upside down to be used. Don't forget to do this, or everything will be in the wrong place! Peg the template in place and then cut around it into the turf using a sharp spade. Tilt the blade back and forth as you go to expose the soil, making it possible to see where you are cutting. Then mark the positions of the shelves.

Now take the depth measurements and add 5 cm/2 in to each one. Excavate the hole to necessary depths, making the shelves the correct width and following the slits that mark out their shape so you can achieve the correct shape for the bottom. Use a spirit level to ensure that both sides of the excavation are at the same height. When you think you have got it right, put the liner in place, check the levels from rim to rim in several places, make any adjustments and then line the excavation with a 5 cm/2 in deep compacted layer of sand. Take out a shallow trench around the perimeter of the pool, about 10 cm/4 in wide. Fill with compacted sand, working it well under the edge of the pool to provide good support. Finish off the edges with either pavers cemented into place or a mixture of gravel and pebbles. Position the plants in containers on the shelves or the bottom of the pond.

BELOW: Pavers disguise the edge of moulded pool liners.

WATERFALLS

WATERFALLS CAN BE MADE using either flexible liners or rigid liners shaped to make a cascade. The advantage of the former is that you can make the pools on each level exactly the shape and size you desire, whereas with a rigid liner you are restricted to what is available in the ranges on sale. You will also need a pump to move the water from the head or top of the waterfall to its foot or bottom. The size of the head and the width and depth of the pools at each level will determine how large a pump you need. Once you have designed the waterfall and know roughly what these measurements will be, ask the supplier of the pump to advise you; be sure to buy one big enough – extra outlay to get things right at the start is a good investment.

Use separate pieces of flexi-liner to make each pool, digging out the lowest one first. The base of subsequent higher pools should incline towards the back so that there is always water in each pool. Cushion the excavated hole just as you would for a straightforward pool, and then spread out the liner on each level, beginning with the lowest pool, so that it completely overlaps the base of the next highest pool. The result will be that each level has a double thickness of liner on the base of the pool and the drop or riser from pool to pool. This gives added durability since the shallow water of this sort of feature gives the liner much more exposure to ultraviolet rays.

Waterfalls made from rigid liners consist of a series of lipped basins that are designed to overlap each other. You should first excavate the hole for the lowest pool, and then proceed as you would for a rigid-lined pool, keeping the levels straight at the sides, and ensuring each level fits snugly over the one beneath, with the lip of the basin overhanging the one below by about one-third its width.

With both sorts of waterfall, the pump and pipe are fitted last and the edges of the liners disguised by rock or slab trims as described earlier.

ABOVE: The overhanging lip of each successive basin is clearly seen in this waterfall, made up of three pools.

RIGHT: Too good to be true? A beautiful creation by a skilled gardener – such as this artificial waterfall – can rival Mother Nature's handiwork.

HALF-BARREL CONTAINER WATER GARDEN

CONTAINERS MADE OF terra cotta or plastic are available from specialist water plant nurseries, along with the sealants you may wish to use to protect the wood of a half whisky barrel.

Half barrels are readily available at nurseries and garden centres. When making your choice look for quality; see that the staves are not split, that the hoops are firmly in place, that the bottom is even and not split or cracked. Be sure that it has been sawn in half evenly; a jagged, uneven edge will spoil the look of the finished water feature.

It will be necessary to clean and soak out any impurities that might leach from the barrel into the water, otherwise these could damage plants and any fish you may wish to house in the container. Use a stiff wire brush on the exterior of the barrel to scrub away rust on the hoops, and any dirt residue inside the barrel. You may be pleasantly surprised by the whiff of whisky as you work; however the next stage will help to clear the air.

The interior of the barrel does not need any protective coating; the charring process done by the cooper takes care of that. Stand the barrel in a shady corner and fill the barrel with water. If it is in good condition it should not leak. There may be some seepage but by keeping the water level topped up on a daily basis the wood will swell and perfect the seal. This soaking process should take a week or so, drawing the whisky residue from the wood. Siphon off the dirty water when complete.

Rainfall will top up a barrel in the garden. To keep the water level steady, drill a hole 2 cm/¾ in in diameter just above the water line.

Choose the site for the barrel carefully. Once it is filled with water, it is an immovable object! Where you place it depends on what you wish to grow; some plants, such as water lilies, like full sun, others need shade. Also, use a spirit level to check that the barrel is level on the ground.

To plant a container use basket pots to house the plants. It is easy to raise the baskets to the desired height for each plant, and they can be easily removed to over winter. A container water garden warms up quickly in the summer sun and chills rapidly (and can freeze over) in the winter. You can offset these effects to a degree by sinking the barrel into the ground so that only a small lip protrudes above the surrounding level of the patio or garden. If you choose to do this, the principle is the same as preparing the site for a rigid liner, only make the hole 5 cm/2 in shallower than the exterior depth of the barrel (since the bottom is usually recessed). Also, be sure to locate the barrel where you won't be in danger of tripping over the exposed rim.

ABOVE: Even goldfish can be kept in a half-barrel container.

RIGHT: This raised pond features *Typha minima*, *Nymphaea pygmaea* **'Helvola', and** *Nymphaea pygmaea* **'Rubra'.**

BELOW: Copying this little garden is a way to bring water features to the garden of a flat's balcony or a narrow patio.

CONCRETE POOLS

THIS IS THE POINT where I would call in the professionals to do the work, but if you really feel the urge to mix and mash, then keep your pool project small and simple. There are a few basic rules to remember.

Gravity will bring the concrete slithering down if you attempt to build anything more than a shallow slope for the pool's sides.

Anything set in concrete needs good foundations, so be sure to site the pond where you can be sure of a rigidly compacted subsoil that will not shrink, expand or change shape in any other way beneath the pond, causing it to crack.

Be sure to reinforce the sides and bottom of the pool with wire mesh netting, such as chicken wire, sandwiched between the outer skin and the final layer of concrete.

In a large pool constructed by professional contractors they would use the wire grid commonly seen in building work, as well as shuttering to build up the sides.

Concrete contains chemicals harmful to fish and plants, so the pond will have to be painted with a sealant. You can add a coat of primer and another of a rubber-based or liquid-plastic paint to add further protection. The pool will have to be filled and refilled a number of times over a period of five or six weeks to leach out the harmful substances.

ABOVE: *Iris pseudacorus* and **Nymphaea have found a home in this concrete pond built with a brick surround.**

RIGHT: Here a concrete pond had been sunk into the surrounding paving.

PLANTING

THE DIFFERENCE BETWEEN formal and informal planting in a water garden is clear from observation. In the former, the water plants are grown as if on show, often because they are unusual, choice, or have something in their character that distinguishes them from the countryside's native water plants; an informal pond landscape usually features the latter. That is not to say you mustn't mix the two, but a startling red-flowered water lily of exotic origin growing among native rushes would be like a fish out of water. So it is a good idea to choose your plants to suit the water garden's characteristics.

One of the great temptations facing any gardener working with a new range of plants is to try to grow everything you can lay your hands on. But restraint will pay off. An uncomplicated display of a few well-grown varieties is easier on the eye (and pocketbook) than an overcrowded, undiscerning collection. The larger the pool, the more you can grow, but be selective even then. One example of an appealing restrained planting would be one or two really large-scale plants such as *Gunnera manicata* or *Rheum palmatum*. These can be balanced by a carefully placed stand of water iris to line the bank. *Marginal* plants – which grow with their roots in the shallow water around the edge of the pool – such as candelabra primulas and cinnamon fern, shelter beneath the umbrella-like leaves of the *Gunnera*. A scented carpet of water mint welcomes you to the water's edge, from where you are able to enjoy a view of the pool itself and the simple assortment of submerged plants – water hyacinths and water dropwort – as several medium-sized water lilies float their leaves and flowers on the water surface.

ABOVE: Skunk cabbage leaves can reach 90 cm/3 ft high.

RIGHT: Water hyacinths should overwinter in a greenhouse.

LEFT: The skunk cabbage is a good choice to grow at the edge of a pool. The reflective surface of the water will enhance the handsome leaves.

BELOW: To some eyes, this pool might be a little crowded. The surface of the pond, beyond the closely-packed marginal plants, is almost solidly covered by water lilies.

Another reason to avoid installing too many plants is that some can grow quite large; there are water lilies that will cover up to 4 sq m/12 sq ft of water surface – that is a lot of plant. Aim to have only about 70 per cent of the total surface of the pool covered with mature plants in a mix of water lilies and other sorts. Planting along the water's edge can be done to exploit the reflective surface of the water by selecting plants for their foliage effect. Contrast long, whippy sword-shaped leaves with rounded shapes; or mix filmy ferns and broad shiny fronds from skunk cabbage and arums; the elegance of groups of beautifully leafed plants can be enhanced by their mirror images glimmering back at you.

LEFT: *Veronica beccabunga* is a useful plant for hiding the edges of your pool.

RIGHT: Yellow flag iris is a familiar marginal water garden plant. You'll find it best suited to large pools.

Practicalities of Planting

Aquatic plants Artificial pools were once created with a layer of soil in the bottom in which the plants were rooted directly; in large pools, aquatics, water lilies and submerged plants were anchored to rocks or bricks and hurled into the water, in the hope that they would take root where they sank! This was not always satisfactory for pool hygiene and the health of the plants themselves. But aquatic plants must be rooted in soil, with their leaves and flowers floating on the water surface. Today, there are specially-designed container baskets in which the plants are rooted into prepared composts formulated for use in water gardens, and so balanced for plant and pool health. Do not on any account be tempted to use ordinary potting composts; the peat or other fibrous matter they contain makes them far too light to withstand constant submersion. Furthermore, peat-based composts would raise the acidity level of the water, having an adverse effect on some plants, but causing more trouble for fish. If you regard water as the growing medium equivalent to the soil in a garden, it too can be tested for its pH, which is the level of acidity. Testing kits for pH can be obtained from garden centres. A pH of 7 is about neutral. A lower figure indicates an acid content; the soil becomes progressively more alkaline the higher the pH is above 7. A reading between 5.5 and 6.5 is acceptable, but if your water is too acid or too alkaline, it can be adjusted by using chemical additives formulated to correct pH.

Another advantage of planting aquatics in baskets is that it makes it possible to adjust the depth at which the plant grows, simply by standing the basket on blocks. These can then be removed gradually until the top growth floats easily on the water surface while the roots in the container rest snugly on the bottom. It is necessary to do this as young plants fresh from the nursery will not be tall enough to reach the surface of the pool.

When plants arrive from the nursery stand them in a bucket of water to prevent the roots drying out. Line the planting basket with a layer of

ABOVE: This water lily is being planted in a container.

38

horticultural textile or hessian sacking; this stops the potting mix from falling into the water. Put a layer of potting compost in the bottom of the planting basket, spread the roots of the plant across the surface of the compost and then fill to within 5 cm/2 in of the basket rim, but take care that the crown of the plant is buried only slightly lower than it was in the nursery; you should be able to discern this from a mark on the stems. Water the container thoroughly, leaving it to soak for an hour or two to be sure that the compost is saturated. Put a layer of washed gravel over the compost.

Lower the basket into the pool and adjust the height of the basket with blocks so that the leaves are floating on the surface. Marginal plants resting on shelves are planted in the same manner and positioned so that their leaves are above the surface of the water. Submerged plants are placed in their planting baskets directly on the bottom of the pool. Floating plants are simply lowered into the water; they do not require soil and baskets. Allow one root per container; don't overcrowd.

Submerged plants All pools must contain submerged oxygenating plants at a rate of at least one healthy clump per two square feet of water surface. These plants exist on sunlight and the nutrients present in the water and provide competition for algae, which left unchecked by such oxygenators would turn the water into pea soup. Submerged plants also benefit fish not only by providing shady shelter but also by exchanging their oxygen for the carbon dioxide produced by the fish.

BELOW: The flower of the skunk cabbage.

Most of these plants are rooted in soil like aquatics, but, as you might suspect from their categorical name, they grow entirely under water and should be planted into baskets as described above, then positioned directly on the bottom of the pool. There is no need, however, to raise or lower the height of the basket with blocks. As the plants mature, the baskets can be removed and the roots divided or cuttings taken from the plants to increase or renew stocks. But keep the more vigorous sorts in check by cutting them back occasionally.

Floating plants This group of plants perform a largely cosmetic role, providing, like annuals or biennials in a land garden, additional but non-permanent cover on the water surface; again, the category describes the plants. They are not anchored by their roots, but float freely in the water absorbing nutrients as they drift. They have the potential to be quite inva-sive. In their countries of origin, many are. But since most are species drawn from the warm waters of tropical countries, they pose little threat in cool British water. They include the lovely water hyacinth which hails from the equatorial regions of the Americas. There it is an invasive weed. In cool temperate climates, however, the winter cold can kill it, and gardeners trying to grow it in Britain have to overwinter their plants in frost-free conditions if they wish them to survive.

Marginal plants Some of the prettiest plants for water gardens are in this category, so try to accommodate a few in your plan. They are mostly perennials and are treated in much the same fashion as land garden peren-nials, only they grow with their roots in the shallow water around the edge of the pool, and must never be allowed to dry out. Each marginal has its own preferred depth of planting and this distance (between the

ABOVE: Water lilies benefit from lifting and dividing, choosing only the strongest growths for replanting, every couple of years.

BELOW: The umbrella-like leaves of *Cyperus alternifolius* make it quite a striking marginal plant.

water surface and the top of the root ball) should be carefully observed; most are planted between 5 cm/2 in deep. The correct depth should be indicated when you purchase the plant.

Unless you have constructed the pool with a variety of levels around the edges, to achieve the correct elevation it will be necessary to plant the marginals into separate containers (one species to a pot, please), and stand the pots on supports as described earlier. As the plants grow they can be lifted and divided to increase and renew stocks. Tidy up the plants every so often to avoid rotting vegetation falling into the water.

Bog plants Strictly speaking, these are not water plants, but they do form an important peripheral group of plants to enhance your planting palette. These are perennials that require a high level of moisture around their roots, doing well only in soil that is constantly damp, but which is not in any way sodden and airless; some bog plants cross over into the marginal category and vice versa. Many moisture-loving herbaceous plants common to the flower border will be useful in a bog garden.

Bog plants are planted directly into the soil and require the same maintenance as land garden perennials. If your bog garden is created by extending the liner from the pond into the soil around it, remember to be careful when digging or weeding with garden hand-forks or cultivators; while a few evenly spaced drainage holes in the liner are necessary, great rips would be going too far!

CARE AND MAINTENANCE

SNAILS, IRIS SAWFLY LARVAE, CADDIS FLIES, leaf miners, aphids, water lily beetles and mosquito larvae all find pools and plants attractive habitats. One of the best ways to control these pests is to have a healthy stock of fish and frogs; their daily feasting will keep the balance of nature tilted in your favour. If you notice pests infesting the surface of foliage where fish can't reach, use a gentle spray of clean water to wash them into the pool. If you feel you must use an insecticide, obtain one that is specifically for water gardens and formulated not to damage fish and beneficial pond life.

Algae poses another problem. In the first few weeks, while the plants are establishing themselves, an alga bloom will appear. This is perfectly normal and should vanish once the balance is established. In several more weeks it should disperse, but the water will never again be completely clear. If the presence of algae drives you to distraction, use a garden rake to scoop it out of the water. But try not to be too fussy; let the pool care for itself and don't be tempted to clean it out every season. To do so would disturb the balance even further, unsettle plants and generally set things back. If it becomes necessary to have a clean out – perhaps the water has become polluted by falling leaves, grass clippings or children chucking biscuits, bread crusts and foreign objects into the water – do so in mid to late spring when the plants have resumed growth and fish have come out of hibernation.

When spring-cleaning a pond, all the plants must be removed and stored carefully, preferably in a shady spot, to preserve their roots. The fish should be transferred to a large container holding some of the old pond water. Choose a warm day in mid to late spring to do the job. Siphon out the water by holding a length of hose beneath the surface so that it fills with water. When it stops bubbling, seal one end with your finger, lift that end out of the pool, remove your finger and the water should come running out of the hose. Use a weak dilution of mild detergent to scrub down the walls of the liner. You will have to rinse and drain the pool

ABOVE: The frog – a natural pest-control system, thanks to their appetite for insects

RIGHT: When cleaning a pond, you will have to rinse and drain the pool several times to wash away the detergent.

several times to disperse the detergent residue. Refill the pond with clean tap water.

Other jobs for spring include lifting and dividing mature aquatic plants that are beginning to outgrow their baskets. Treat them just as you would garden perennials, only take care that the roots do not dry out.

During later spring, throughout summer and during the winter, herons pose a big threat to fish; these birds seem to have radar direction, swooping on ponds and scooping out the best of your Koi with remarkable accuracy. Some people swear by a heron statue standing sentry at the pool edge; the interlopers think the territory has already been claimed. Some water gardeners stretch netting across the pool, and a few take the trouble to fix it just below the water's surface. This has the advantage of partially concealing the netting; I find that few things interfere more with the enjoyment of a water garden than a blanket of netting, but it is a

ABOVE: Scoop algae and unwanted pond weed out of the water by using an ordinary garden rake.
BELOW: This pond heater has been installed during the autumn, before the first frosts.

necessary evil. If you settle on this method, be sure that the netting is not so far below the surface that it interferes with fish rising to feed and take in oxygen. Herons need to stand at the water's edge or be able to walk into it; an alternative, less intrusive method is a string of fine black nylon thread around the perimeter about 45 cm/18 in high from the ground to catch the birds at about knee level, and so interferes with their access.

Year-round maintenance is very much the same as for the flower garden. During the summer pay attention to water levels in pool and bog gardens, topping up and watering when necessary. Feed plants in the early part of the season to encourage healthy growth using a proprietary fertiliser specifically for water plants. Feed fish regularly, too.

As the year fades to autumn, dead-head plants by removing faded blossoms. Keep pool and plants tidy by removing wilting and dying foliage. Any plants that have given up the ghost should be removed now rather than later, when they have begun to rot and pollute the water.

LEFT: This large net umbrella, a striking contraption, will keep leaves and herons out.

If leaves blow into the pond from nearby plantings, you can screen the pond with a canopy of fine netting, rather like the old-fashioned muslin umbrellas used to cover food at picnics. Doing this will save you a daily chore of raking leaves from the pond.

Tender and half-hardy exotic water plants should be removed now and moved to the shelter of a frost-free greenhouse.

BELOW: Use a pan of hot water to melt a hole in the ice. But hold on to it!

ABOVE: **A thin layer of ice has formed on top of this Nottinghamshire pond during a February cold spell.**

During the winter your main concern will be to keep the pool from freezing over. This is essential if there are fish in the pond, and could also prevent damage to rigid liners and concrete pools since water expands when it freezes; the pressure created by the expansion could cause the liners to crack. You can purchase water heaters that float on the surface of the water keeping a smallish area free of ice. One heater is sufficient to keep an ice-free space in a pond of up to 4.5 sq m/50 sq ft. You can also stand a pan or kettle of boiling water on the ice until it melts through – keep hold of the pan though! If there are no fish, floating a child's large rubber ball in the water might be enough to absorb the pressure of expanding ice; use several in a large pool.

Safety

Quite apart from the safety precautions you must take when including electric pumps, filters, lights and so on as part of the water garden, there is one other, highly critical safety consideration: *water plus small children is an accident waiting to happen.* Where there are children about, you cannot be too careful. Put a good fence around any pool, so matter how small. Remember, it is possible to drown in a puddle.

Water Garden Plants

A WORD TO THE WISE: *do not ever* take a wild water plant from its native habitat. It may be tempting to stock your water garden for free, but there is a price to pay in damaged natural landscapes and heavy fines if you are caught. Always buy your plants from a reputable nursery. They can give you expert advice and steer you clear of costly mistakes – for example, accidentally introducing rampant or invasive water weeds such as greater duckweed (*Spirodella polyrhiza*). The plants here are indexed according to their Latin species names.

RIGHT: **Primulas, irises and hostas in a bog garden.**

BELOW: *Acorus calamus* **'Variegatus'**

BOTTOM: *Alisma plantago-aquatica*

Acorus gramineus
Sweet sedge
SUBMERGED OR MARGINAL
h 25 cm/10 in s to 25 cm/10 in
A semi-evergreen grass-like plant with stiff narrow fragrant eaves which were once gathered as a 'strewing herb'. The cultivar 'Variegatus' has cream variegation on the green leaves. Full sun.

Alisma plantago-aquatica
Water Plantain
MARGINAL
h to 75 cm/30 in s to 45 cm/18 in
This is an herbaceous perennial for the bog garden or for planting at the water's edge. It has broad leaves beneath a frothy foam of pale pink flowers like an exceptionally delicate gypsophila. Full sun.

Aponogeton distachyos
Water hawthorn
FLOATING
s to 1.2m/4 ft
This perennial floating plant sheds its lozenge-shaped leaves in autumn to reappear in the spring. A flush of white fragrant flowers are present all summer. Full sun and deep water.

Azolla Caroliniana
Fairy Moss
FLOATING

s indefinite

Perennial fern for sun or partial shade: in shade the colour is blue-green, becoming more red in the sunlight.

Butomus umbellatus
Flowering rush
MARGINAL

h 1m/3 ft s 45 cm/18 in

Perennial with narrow, strappy green leaves and dainty umbels of pale pink flowers in summer. Full sun.

Calla palustris
Bog arum
MARGINAL

h 30 cm/12 in s 45 cm/18 in

Perennial with semi-evergreen, heart-shaped flat leaves and large white spathes, followed by a spike of orangey-red berries. This spreads slowly and looks good contrasted with narrow-leafed marginals. Full sun.

Caltha leptosepala
MARGINAL

h 30 cm/12 in s 15 cm/10 in

Perennial with small glossy heart-shaped leaves and buttercup-like flowers with white petals around a boss of golden of stamens. Full sun.

ABOVE: Hostas (in foreground) and primulas

Caltha palustris
Marsh marigold
MARGINAL

h 45 cm/18 in s to 60 cm/24 in

Glossy green leaves with a rather more rounded heart shape than the species above, set off the equally glossy bright buttercup-yellow flowers. A perennial for the water's edge, it flowers in the spring. Full sun.

The cultivar 'Flore Pleno' has bunches of vividly coloured double flowers, but the plant is slightly smaller, h and s to 25 cm/10 in. Full sun.

Carex pseudocyperus

MARGINAL OR BOG

h 50 cm-1m/20-36 in

A grassy plant with long tapering yellow-green leaves and dangling inflorescences that look like hazel catkins. Full sun. *C. stricta* 'Bowles' Golden' grows to 45 cm/18 in, and has bright yellow-green foliage.

Ceratophyllum demersum
Hornwort
SUBMERGED

Bottle brush-like leaves surround the floating stems; as cold weather settles in the plant withdraws into the pool, undergoing a sort of hibernation on the floor. As the water warms up again in spring, it rises up again out of the water.

Eichhornia crassipes
Water hyacinth
FLOATING
h 25 cm/10 in s invasive in good conditions
Evergreen plant with fleshy broad leaves and spikes of scented lilac purple flowers during summer. This is not hardy so must be over wintered in frost-free conditions. Full sun.

Elodea crispa (see *Lagarosiphon major*)

Fontinalis anipyretica
Willow moss
SUBMERGED
s indefinite
An oxygenator with fronds of small green leaves, its name describes its effect perfectly. Provides dense cover for spawning fish. Grows in full sun or dense shade and anywhere in–between.

ABOVE: *Caltha palustris* **with skunk cabbage**

BELOW: *Iris laevigata* **'Variegata'**

BOTTOM: *Hottuynia cordata*

Hosta spp. and var.
Plantain lily
BOG
h 12-60 cm/4-24 in s 15-90 cm/6-35 in dependent on variety
This is the familiar foliage plant common to woodland gardens, flower borders and any other suitable spot where the soil is moist. There are dozens of different sorts with variegated foliage, huge round leaves, tiny tapering spear-like leaves, smooth leaves or deeply ridged. This variety makes them useful to provide contrast and texture to bog garden and pool-side planting schemes. Full sun or part shade.

Hottonia palustris
Water violet
SUBMERGED
s indefinite
Does best in lime-free water in part shade, where it will produce masses of the delicate flower spikes that rise up to 30 cm/12 in above the water from the submerged, finely-toothed leaf fronds.

Houttuynia cordata 'Chamaeleon'
MARGINAL
h 12.5cm (5in) s indefinite
Aromatic citrus-scented heart-shaped leaves are splashed with cream and pink with simple white flowers in summer. Partial shade.

ABOVE: *Caltha palustris* '**Flore peno**'

BELOW: *Butomus umbellatus*

Hydrocharis morsus-ranae
Frog bit
FLOATING
s to 1m/3 ft
A pretty little thing for small pools, it has three-petalled white flowers in summer held above the rosettes of kidney-shaped leaves.

Iris pseudoacorus
Yellow flag
MARGINAL OR BOG
h 90 cm/3 ft s 60 cm/2 ft
The common yellow-flowered iris of ditches and natural ponds. The cultivars 'Bastardii' and 'Beuron' have softer yellow colouring. 'Variegatus' has white flashes on the foliage. Full sun or part shade.

Lagarosiphon major
SUBMERGED
s indefinite
A semi-evergreen oxygenating plant that spreads to form a thicket of snake-like fronds floating beneath the water surface. Will need thinning periodically to check rampant growth. Full sun.

LEFT: *Menyanthes trifoliata*

Lobelia cardinalis
Cardinal flower
BOG

h 90 cm/3 ft s 60 cm/2 ft

Because of the dark red colouring of the foliage and the crimson flowers, this is an excellent plant to provide counterpoint to a generally green water planting scheme Slightly tender, so if in doubt mulch well or take cuttings. Part shade.

Lysichitum americanum
Skunk cabbage
MARGINAL OR BOG

h 1m/3 ft s 1m/3 ft

One of the more architectural plants for a dramatic display. The broad tapering leaves unfurl in early spring followed by bright yellow flowers, the spathes looking like the hood of a cobra. Needs plenty of space to look at its best. Full sun.

BELOW: *Lobelia cardinalis*

Mentha x piperita
Peppermint
BOG

h30cm (12in) s 60cm (2ft)

The familiar mint of the herb garden thrives in the wet conditions by the water's edge. Full sun or part shade.

ABOVE: *Myostis scorpioides*

Menyanthes trifolata
Bogbean
MARGINAL
h up to 30 cm/1 ft s 25 cm/10 in
Three-lobed leaves reminiscent of broad bean leaves, and white flowers make this an attractive and well-behaved plant for the water's edge.

BELOW: *Rheum palmatum* '**Atrosanguinem**'

Myosotis scorpioides
Water forget-me-not
MARGINAL
h 16 cm/6 in s 30 cm/12 in
Very like the flower garden forget-me-not, except the small green leaves are glossy and it flowers thoughout the summer. Will grow in wet soil or shallows. Full sun.

Myriophyllum verticilliatum
Water milfoil
SUBMERGED
s indefinite
Khaki green leaves in whorls along the submerged stems. It is deciduous but bursts into leaf again in the spring. Full sun.
The species *M. aquaticum*, also known as Parrot's feather, is more tender but with a softer colouring; the glaucous foliage turns a pleasing autumnal red before fading for winter.

Nuphar lutea
Yellow water lily; Brandy bottle
AQUATIC
s 1.5m/5 ft
An extremely vigorous perennial with globular yellow flowers and leathery, round green leaves. It will quickly colonise a pool. Prefers partial shade.

Nymphea species and varieties
Water lilies
AQUATIC
Height and spread; in this case height refers to the depth at which the water lily grows, measured from the top of the container to the leaves resting on the water. Some water gardeners maintain that the spread of a water lily will be equal to or half again as much as the depth at which it grows best. So to choose a water lily for a container, look for one requiring little depth of water, i.e. a short distance between the top of the container and the leaf resting on the water surface. Be cautious about introducing anything requiring more than 45–60 cm/18–24 in of depth, as it will probably be too vigorous for an artificial pool, but fine to grow in a large natural pond. All water lilies like full sun.

Dwarf varieties and cultivars for 10–30 cm/4–12 in
N. pygmaea 'Alba' produces its tiny flowers 2.5 cm/1 in across, over a long period; it does best in only 10 cm/4 in of water. 'Helvola' is equally dainty, but with bright golden-yellow flowers.
'Aurora', 'Graciella' and 'Indiana' are dwarf with flowers in shades of coppery pink and orange.
N. odorata 'W.B. Shaw' has pale pink scented flowers; 'Laydekeri Liliacea' has flowers fading from carmine red to shell pink as they age. 'Froebellii' has rich crimson red flowers; 'James Brydon' has cherry pink flowers.

ABOVE: *Nymphaea pygmaea* 'Helvola'.

BELOW: *Nymphaea* 'Firecrest'

Varieties and cultivars for 30-60 cm/12-24 in

'Marliacea Albida' is a popular white-flowered variety; its sister 'Marliacea Rosea' has pink flowers and is one of the few water lilies that will tolerate shade. 'Rose Arey' has buff pink flowers; the bright yellow flowers of 'Sunrise' open early in the day – hence the name.

Vigorous lilies for up to 1m/3 ft

'Marliacea Chromatella' is slightly tender; *N. alba* is one of the strongest growers, as is 'Gladstoniana'.

BELOW: Only large pools are suited to the most vigorous water lilies

Nymphoides peltata
Fringed water lily
AQUATIC

s 60 cm/24 in

A sturdy plant for the wildlife pond, it is has round green leaves often flecked with brown and small yellow flowers. Full sun.

Orontium aquaticum
Golden club
MARGINAL TO AQUATIC

s 60 cm/24 in

Snaky little flower spikes rise above the broad, tapering leaves in early spring. Can be quite vigorous so give plenty of space. Full sun.

BELOW: *Pontederia cordata*

ABOVE: *Orontium aquaticum*

Osmunda cinnamomea
Cinnamon fern
BOG

1–1.2m/3–4 ft

Many of the species within this genus enjoy boggy conditions, but the cinnamon fern with its curiously fragrant foliage is especially striking. Full sun or part shade.

Pontederia cordata
Pickerel weed
MARGINAL OR AQUATIC

h 75 cm/30 in s 45 cm/18 in

Perennial plant with spikes of forget-me-not blue flowers that bloom in late summer showing up beautifully against the inky green, broad tapering leaves. Full sun.

Potamogeton crispus
Curled pondweed
SUBMERGED

s indefinite

An oxygenator for cool deep water. The fronds look very like seaweed, glossy with crimped edges.

Primula japonica
Candlelabra primula
BOG

h 30–60 cm/12–24 in s 30–45 cm/12–18 cm
Clump-forming perennial with rosettes of crinkly green leaves and tall
flower spikes bearing whorls of blossom in shades of white, mauve,
carmine and pink. Full sun or part shade.

Rheum palmatum
Ornamental rhubarb
BOG

h 2m/6 ft s 1.5m/5 ft
This perennial rivals the gunnera for sheer size. The leaves are lobed and
deeply ribbed looking very similar to edible rhubarb. The cultivar
'Atrosanguineum' has deep wine-red tinted foliage and stems. Full sun.

Sagittaria latifolia
American arrowhead
MARGINAL

h 1.5m/5 ft s 60 cm/2 ft
Perennial plant has soft green leaves shaped liked arrowheads with pani-
cles of small white flowers through summer. Full sun.

RIGHT: *Zantesdeschia aethiopica*

BELOW: *Stratiotes aloides*

Saururus cernuus
Lizard's tail, Water dragon
BOG OR MARGINAL
h 25cm/10 in s 30 cm/12 in
Arrowhead-shaped leaves support the white flower racemes which appear in summer. Full sun.

Scirpus tabernaemontani 'Zebrinus'
Zebra rush
MARGINAL
h to 1.5m/6 ft s 1.2m/4 ft
A non-invasive relative of the bulrush, this has variegated rush-like leaves that are striped creamy white. Because of its size it needs plenty of room, but will grow in very shallow water. Full sun.

Stratiotes aloides
Water soldier
FLOATING, SUBMERGED
s 30 cm/12 in
Rosettes of khaki green leaves have a spiky texture; in summer there are small white flowers dotted around the foliage. Full sun.

Typha latifolia
Cat tail
MARGINAL
h to 2.5 m/8 ft s 60 cm/2 ft
This the common rush seen in wet ditches and natural ponds. It is very invasive and so not suitable to growing anywhere except large water gardens. Full sun.

Zantedeschia aethiopica
Arum lily
MARGINAL OR BOG
h to 1m/39 in
A garden perennial for moist soil or in water to 30 cm/1 ft deep. Easy to propagate from offsets taken in winter.'Green Goddess' has green spathes – quite eye-catching in the garden.

ABOVE: *Typha latifolia* **'Variegata'**

INDEX

(References to photographs are indicated by *italics*.)

Animal life: Fish, 12, 13, *22*, 30, 32, 38, 40, 44, 47, 49;
 Frogs, 44, *44*;
 Herons, protection from, 46

Bog gardens, 24, *24*, *25*, 43;
 See also Plants: species and varieties

Containers: as a pond garden, 30, *38*;
 for aquatic plants in a pond, 38-40;
 for submerged plants in a pond, 40-41

Digging/excavating: of informal ponds, 20-21;
 for waterfalls, 28

Extras for pools, 14-19;
 Fountains, 8, 14, *14*, *15*, *16,* 17, 18, *18*, *19*;
 Heaters, *48*, 49;
 Lighting, 18;
 Waterfalls, 8, 14, 26, 28-29

Liners: bedding for, 22-23, 24, 27;
 flexible, 8, 20;
 for bog gardens, 24;
 material of, 20;
 repair of, 23;
 rigid, 8, 26

Pests and diseases, 44-49;
 and insecticide, 44;
 greater duckweed, 50

Plants: and fertiliser, 47;
 aquatic, 12, 38;
 bog plants, 43;
 exotic, 48;
 floating, 12, 42;
 lifting and dividing, *43*, 46;
 marginal, *39*, 40, 42, *42*;
 oxygenators, 40;
 submerged, 12, 40;
 toxic, 13;
 types of, 12;
 wild, 50;
 year-round maintenance, 47

Plants: species and varieties, *see overleaf*

Pools/ponds: clearing and drainage, 44-46;
 concrete, 32, 33;
 design, 10-13, 32-43, *37*;
 edging, 22-23, 24, 27;
 filling with water, 22;
 formal, 8;
 ice and frost, 30, 47, *47*, 48, 49;
 informal, 8, 20;
 maintenance, 47;
 netting, 46-47, *46*, 48, *48*;
 paper template for, 26;
 safety, 49;
 sealant and protection, 32;
 shape of, 8, 11;
 size of, 12-13;
 wire mesh, 32

Pumps, 14, 28

Soil: acidity, 39;
 choice of, 38;
 disposal of, 11-12

Tools: brush, 30;
 carpenter's level, 22, 26, 30;
 Garden hose, 20, 44;
 Spade, 20, 26, 43

Picture Acknowledgments

The work of the following photographers has been used:
David Askham: 14(b); **John Baker**: 32, 36; **Clive Boursnell**: 6, 22, 51(c); **Lynne Brotchie**: 11; **Linda Burgess**: 14(t); **Brian Carter**: 48(b), 54(t); **Bob Challinor**: 24(t), 56(b); **Densey Clyne**: 56(t); **Geoff Dawn**: 28, 38(t); **David England**: 50(t), 51(b); **Ron Evans**: 13; **Christopher Fairweather**: 35, 59; **John Glover**: i, ii, 10(b); 16, 18(t), 25, 26, 29, 41, 47, 52(t); **Tim Griffith**: 18(b); **Sunniva Harte**: 49, 52(c), 60, 62; **Marijke Heuff**: 33; **Michael Howes**: 38(b), 43, 44, 45(b); **Lamontagne**: 15, 24(b), 30; **Jane Legate**: 7, 12(b), 45(t), 46(b); **John Miller**: 42; **Clive Nichols**: 9, 53(c); **Howard Rice**: 31, 40, 46(t), 56(c); **Gary Rogers**: 20; **J.S. Sira**: 8, 10(t), 17, 19, 37, 39, 51(t), 54(b), 58; **Ron Sutherland**: 7, 12(t), 48(t); **Brigitte Thomas**: 21, 23, 27; **Juliette Wade**: 55(b); **Didier Willery**: 52(b), 53(b), 55(t); **Steven Wooster**: 50(b), 57, 61.

The following designers worked on some of the photographed material:
Cedar Design: 7; **Hampstead Horticultural Society**: 9; **Ry Nowell**: 28; **Duane Paul Design Team**: 12(t); **Mien Ruys**: 33.

The following gardens were phtographed:
Bakers Farm, Sussex, England: 8; **Hadspen House**: 37; **Hollington Herbs, Berkshire, England**: 19; **Lake Naivasha, Kenya**: 35.

PLANTS: SPECIES AND VARIETIES

(References to photographs are indicated by *italics*.)

Acorus calamus, 48, *48*
Acorus gramineus (Sweet sedge), 48
Alisma plantago-aquatica (Water plantain), 48, 57;
Aponogeton distachyos (Water hawthorn), 48, *51*;
Astilbes, *23*, *51*
Azolla Caroliniana, 50, *51*

Butomus umbellatus (Flowering rush), 50

Calla palustris (Bog arum), 50, *52*
Caltha leptosepala, 50; *C. palustris* (Marsh marigold), 26, 50, *53*
Carex pseudocyperus, 51; *C. Stricta*, 51
Ceratophyllum demersum (Hornwort), 51
Cyperus alternifolius, *41*, 56

Duckweed, 12, 48

Eichhornia crassipes (Water hyacinth), 34, *35*, 40, 52
Elephant weed, *23*
Elodea, 12

Fontinalis anipyretica (Willow moss), 52

Gunnera manicata, 24, 34

Hostas sp., 24, *50*, 52; and var., 26, 58
Hottonia palustris (Water violet), 52
Houttuynia cordata, 52, *52*
Hydrocharis morsus-ranae (Frog bit), 53

Iris laevigata, *52*; *I. pseudoacorus* (Yellow flag iris) 24, 32, *32*, *39*, 44, 53

Lagarosiphon major (*E. crispa*), 53
Ligularia, 24
Lobelia cardinalis (Cardinal flower), 54, *54*
Lysichitum americanum (Skunk cabbage), *34*, 36, 37, 54

Mentha x piperita, 54

Menyanthes trifolata, *54*, 55
Miscanthus sp, 24
Myriophyllum aquaticum, 55; *M. verticilliatum* (Water milfoil), 57
Mysotis scorpioides (Water forget-me-not), 55, *55*

Nuphar lutea (Yellow water lily; Brandy bottle), 56
Nymphaea sp., 12, *21*, 25, *26*, *32*, 37, 40, 56, *56*, 57, 60;
    and var., 26, 58;
    N. alba, 57;
    N. laydekeri fulgens, *56*;
    N. odorata, 56;
    N. pygmaea, 30, 56, *56*
Nymphoides peltata (Fringed water lily), 58;

Orontium aquaticum (Golden club), 58, *59*
Osmunda cinnamomea (Cinnamon fern), 24, 34, 59

Pontamogeton crispus (Curled pondweed), 59
Pontederia cordata (Pickerel Weed), *23*, 56, 59
Primula, 52; *P. japonica* (Candlelabra primula), 24, 34, 60

Rheum palmatum (ornamental rhubarb), 24, 34, *55*, 60

Sagittaria latifolia (American arrowhead), 60
Saururus cernuus (Lizard's tail; Water dragon), 62
Scirups tabernaemontani 'Zebrinus' (Zebra rush), 62
Stratiotes aloides (Water soldier), 60, 62

Typha latifolia (Cat tail), 62, *62*

Veronica beccabunga, 38

Water chestnut, 26
Water dropwort, 34
Water iris, 34
Water mint, 34

Zantedeschia aethiopica (Arum lily), *61*, 62